Wake Up Call

Vicki Hallett

Llumina Christian Books

© 2009 Vicki Hallett

All rights reserved. No part of this publication may be reproduced or transmitted in any form or by any means electronic or mechanical, including photocopy, recording, or any information storage and retrieval system, without permission in writing from the copyright owner.

ISBN: 978-1-62550-521-7

Table of Contents

Introduction — i
Preface — v
Acknowledgments — xi

1. The Rapture — 1
2. The Anti-Christ — 5
3. Israel Is Attacked — 11
4. Tribulation Begins — 15
5. Two Witnesses — 23
6. Trumpet Judgments — 29
7. Seal Judgments — 37
8. The Great Tribulation — 45
9. Your Decision — 51
10. The Glorious Appearing — 57
11. Battle of Armageddon — 65

12. *Hope* 71

13. *The Millennium* 75

14. *How It All began* 79

Additional Information and References 85

Introduction

You may be curious about who I am and what inspired me to write this book. First of all, I'd like to state for the record that I'm married to the most wonderful man in the world. I'm sure there are many wives who would argue this point with me, but I feel very blessed to have married my childhood sweetheart. It was many years before we actually married, and I plan to include our love story on my website for those interested. Between us, we have seven children, seventeen grandchildren and – at the time of the writing of this book – an eighteenth on the way.

But our lives have not been total bliss. Besides the regular hardships that all families face, we experienced a terrible tragedy in 2003 when our oldest daughter, Tia, unexpectedly passed away from diabetic complications. She was 28 years old with three small children. I fervently believe that losing a child is the most devastating, heart-wrenching experience a parent can face, and my heart goes out to everyone else who has endured this particular loss. There were times when I truly felt I couldn't face another day or survive the grief that overwhelmed me. Both my parents have passed on and I suffered with each of their deaths, but my grief was multiplied a hundredfold when it was my child. I don't agree with the saying that "time heals all wounds" because there are some wounds that time can never heal. This pain will be with me until the day that I die, but I've learned to deal with it and enjoy the life that God has given me. I have great faith that I will see Tia again and that this time on earth will be very short compared to the time I will have with her in heaven. The knowledge that Tia is there and that our separation is only temporary is what keeps me going. It offers me a sense of peace, even within the pain and sorrow of missing her. Her memorial website is <u>keithandvickihallett.com/tia</u>

I am a reader and would rather curl up with a good book than watch television. So when my daughter passed away, I tried to focus on books that would help me to process my grief. I read stories about how others coped with great losses, along with good literature that I hoped would nourish my mind and soul. I went to a support group and visited a grief counselor, but nothing seemed to help until I subscribed to a monthly newsletter issued by "Broken Hearts, Living Hope" — a Christian support network for grieving families. These newsletters led me to reach out to others who understood the pain I was in. My healing process began when I realized that God gave us this life so that we might do our very best in every situation. He never said we would always have sunshine; and indeed, it is during our times of rain that we learn to reach out and touch others who are suffering. When I stopped dwelling solely on my own circumstances and focused on those of others, I was better able to endure my own pain. I'm not saying I no longer cry over my daughter's death. I still have tearful moments and I always will — as long as I still have breath and memories. But what has helped me the most is all the reading I have done about heaven. I have obsessively studied the Bible and many other books so as to learn more about the place in which my daughter now resides. At one point, while I was reading "Heaven" by Randy Alcorn, I joined a Bible study group led by my pastor and was excited to learn that he was basing our study on the very same book I was reading. It was gratifying to pore over scripture and to achieve a greater understanding of our future home according to the Bible.

After so much reading for the purpose of study, I decided to read something for fun. In general, I am not a fiction reader and would rather read a biography than something made up by an imaginative author. Nevertheless, I found myself picking up the first book in the "Left Behind" series by Tim LaHaye. This exciting and intriguing series offers a vivid depiction of events that could take place after the rapture. I couldn't get enough of these books and went through the series all too quickly. It was almost a disappointment to finish the last book because I was so hooked. Sometimes LaHaye's fictional events would send me straight to the Bible to compare its text with his. I didn't believe that certain events in the series could actually correspond with anything written in scripture. To my continual surprise, I found that every scene conjured by LaHaye was based directly on a Biblical passage.

The bookstore clerk who sold me the first volume remarked that he never read the series because he thought of it as full of "doom and gloom." But my experience of these books was exactly the opposite – reading them made me feel closer to God and reaffirmed my faith in Him.

I became such a lover of the series that I recommended it to a good friend who had lost two sons and a husband in three separate tragedies. She and I exchanged several letters and drew mutual comfort from our friendship and our shared love of God. She decided to read the series and it has changed her life much in the way it changed mine.

Because of my interest in the prophecies of Revelation and other books in the Bible, I've gone on to read the work of other authors such as Hal Lindsey, Beth Moore and Hank Hanegraaf (to mention just a few). Finally, I was inspired to write a book for everyone with a desire to decipher the mysteries of the most difficult book in the Bible. My greatest inspiration has remained Tim LaHaye, for he has the ability to keep the reader spellbound while presenting the material of Revelation in a context that the average person can understand. When the rapture of the church takes place, there will be thousands of people with no opportunity to read all the available books and compare them with scripture. I wanted to offer a guidebook that presented this difficult material in a way that was accessible to everyone.

So this is my gift to you and I pray it will help you to make the right decisions in your life.

Preface

Many times I have picked up the Bible and paged through the last chapter. The book of Revelation. This book might as well have been in another language because I was "lost in translation". You may relate to this experience as many others do. The knowledge the book of Revelation has to offer is very powerful if we can unlock it. It is my hope I can assist you with understanding God's message so you can see how it pertains to your life. The message can be a bit overwhelming and therefore easy to put down and move on to another book that can be easily understood. In our busy world we find it difficult at times to sit, study, and dissect the Bible. My decision to write this book was made to help you for it doesn't matter whether you have never picked up a Bible in your life or whether you are a scholar. God's message is for everyone living on this earth. I am excited that you've decided to read this book. Regardless of whether or not the rapture has yet taken place, it will be a wonderful guide, full of information to help you with your future.

This book is my interpretation of God's message and was written for all people, regardless of spiritual or religious orientation. Perhaps you have heard this message before; perhaps you feel confused, or reluctant to believe it. Whatever your personal circumstances might be, I challenge you to listen to this book's message of hope.

If the rapture has yet to occur, you might be a skeptic. You may doubt that the Bible is the word of God and that the event known as the rapture of the church will really take place. Even if these are your beliefs, please hold on to this book, because it will be very helpful during the aftermath of the rapture.

If the rapture of the church has taken place (described in chapter one), you will most likely be searching for answers about what is happening in the world. This book was inspired by the Bible and will be filled with scripture for your study. But I want to say something very important to you here at the outset:

There is HOPE. YOU CAN STILL FIND PEACE WITH GOD AND MAKE IT TO HEAVEN.

Yes, there is a second chance and I want to encourage you not to waste any time with this decision. Time is of the essence. Catastrophic events will unfold and many people will die. Regardless of where you are in the tribulation period (which will be explained in this book), you can make a decision that will save your soul. Moreover, by sharing this book, you can help others around you.

You may be wondering how a wonderful, loving God could allow such destruction and grief in the world.

To answer that, let me remind you that God is love and God loves you. God wants everyone to turn to Him through his son Jesus Christ. God did not unleash the destruction you are seeing all around you. Satan is responsible, and he wants to destroy and devour all that he can. Satan knows his time is short and he will wreak as much destruction as God will allow. Yes, God allows Satan to destroy. Why?

What kind of God would allow Satan to cause such destruction, agony, grief, and turmoil? The answer: a God who loves us so much that He sacrificed His only son to pay the price for our sins. We all fall very short of the glory of God, and the truth is that no one deserves salvation. So God sent his son, Jesus, to pay the ultimate price so that we might experience salvation and enter heaven (see chapter nine).

God loves us so much that He is going to do everything He can to bring as many people as possible to their knees before him. Think about it for a minute: what kind of person is most likely to come to his knees and seek peace in his life? Would it be someone without a care in the world? Or would it be a person in need of help, guidance and encouragement — someone experiencing agony or grief?

Since we humans were given free will, we can be extremely stubborn. Some of us are so stubborn that we need a "**wake-up call**" to open our eyes, turn us in the direction of our heavenly Father, and help us to acknowledge our need for guidance.

Let's take a moment to revisit the reason we were created. God created us because He wanted a relationship with us, one in which He could enjoy fellowship and bestow blessings. God made the earth for man, who was designed to live forever. When He created the planet, everything was perfect. We were created to eat fruit, nuts and vegetables for nourishment. Since there wasn't to be any killing or death, we were not intended to use animals for food. Nothing bad had been created at that time, in heaven or upon the earth.

God instructed Adam and Eve not to eat of the tree of knowledge of good and evil because He wanted to allow them "free will." His plan was to give them a choice. By doing this, He let man make his own decision. Love and fellowship with God was not to be forced but given freely. Genuine love cannot exist unless it is given by choice. God provided Adam and Eve with a perfect world as well as complete fellowship with Him. They were told they would surely die if they ate of the fruit on that tree. This implies that originally, they were immortal beings.

It wasn't until after the earth was created that Lucifer (God's highest-ranking archangel) was cast out of heaven. In Ezekiel 28:12-14, the Bible states that Lucifer (also known as Satan) was the chief angel and the most brilliant of all beings in heaven. Because of Lucifer's desire to be God and rule all things (including God), he convinced one-third of all the angels to back him in the brief battle that ensued before he was exiled from heaven. God prepared Hades (or Hell) as a place for Lucifer and the angels who followed him. I believe Lucifer's fall from heaven did not occur until after the week of creation described in Genesis 1, because at that time, God pronounced His <u>whole creation</u> "very good" (Genesis 1:31). I don't believe He would have stated that His whole creation was very good after the fall of Satan.

The Bible states that Satan entered the Garden of Eden in the form of a serpent. It is interesting to think about how Eve reacted to a talking serpent. The Bible doesn't tell us that they were surprised when the serpent talked to them; if you've heard this story before, have you ever wondered why they weren't? Do you think the animals in Eden talked? For me, it is amusing to think that they did. The Bible tells us that God once caused a donkey to speak. I would like to think the animals talked in the garden and that they might even talk in heaven.

Satan tempted Adam and Eve by telling them the forbidden fruit would not kill them and they wouldn't die; instead, they would actually gain knowledge of good and evil. Genesis 3:4-5 tells us that he said: *Ye shall not surely die....ye shall be as gods.* At that time, Adam and Eve didn't know what good and evil were. God knew that if they incurred this knowledge, they would be continually tempted toward evil and ultimately separated from Him. Unfortunately, Adam and Eve chose to listen to Satan and disobey God's commandment. By eating the forbidden fruit, they compromised their fellowship with God and submitted to Satan. In doing so, they forfeited the earth to Satan.

Have you asked yourself why Jesus had to die on the cross? Jesus came to redeem the world that God created and gave to man.

Because of sin, people are no longer immortal and eventually die; however, our souls live on. God made us eternal beings. We do not simply cease to exist at death; instead, we can spend eternity with God or in hell. Matthew 25:41 states: *He made us to live with Him forever; and He made hell for the devil and his angels.* There are only two places to go. If we don't choose to be with God, we will be choosing hell.

Jesus' death was brutal. He took on the punishment of every imaginable sin so that everyone might have the opportunity for salvation. Most of us have seen pictures, statues or replicas of Jesus on the cross. What most of these representations fail to reveal is the horrific mutilation of Jesus' body. People don't want to see that. It is quite an emotional experience to consider His pain on the cross. The thorns that crowned Him were forced deep into his head; blood covered His face from the wounds. He was flogged with a lead-tipped whip that ripped the flesh from His body. His back was unrecognizable when they were finished with him. Jesus could have cried out to God at any time and requested release from this punishment. But He chose to purchase our salvation with His own crucifixion.

I hope this helps you understand how the human condition came about and why the earth is in such turmoil today. As I turn now from Genesis to Revelation, we will look into the Bible's depiction of the last days.

The tribulation period will last for only seven years. During this time, many will die without coming to Jesus for salvation (see chapter four).

During this period, God will do everything He can to "wake" people up. It is going to be catastrophic. He is going to allow Satan to bring horrible plagues and destruction to the earth. Throughout this period, thousands of people will turn to Jesus and thousands will not.

There are only two choices, my friend. If you choose not to turn your life over to our wonderful savior Jesus Christ, you will be serving Satan. You cannot make it to heaven by your works alone. You might be a wonderful parent, a pillar of society, a caring spouse and a true friend, but without salvation in Jesus Christ, you will not be going to heaven. Satan will do everything he can to trick and deceive you through the new leaders of the world (see chapter two). DON'T ALLOW THE PEACE TALKS AND LIES TO TEMPT YOU INTO FOLLOWING AND BELIEVING THE NEW WORLD LEADERS.

Whom will you serve? There are only two choices. You cannot serve both.

Acknowledgments

I want to thank my adorable loving husband, Keith, who continually gave me support, encouragement and lots of patience.

I also would like to thank my editor and friend, Elissa Wylde for all the patience and assistance she gave me. I couldn't have done this without her. I want to thank my friends and family for the encouragement, wisdom, and guidance through the journey of writing this book.

COVER PHOTO TAKEN BY: KEITH HALLETT

ANGEL ART DRAWN BY: BRANDI KUSKIE

The Rapture

1 Corinthians 15:52 (New International Version)

^{52}in a flash, in the twinkling of an eye, at the last trumpet. For the trumpet will sound, the dead will be raised imperishable, and we will be changed.

The rapture of the church has been prophesied for centuries. Although the word "Rapture" is not found in the Bible, the event itself is mentioned several times. No one knows when God is going to instruct an angel to sound the trumpet and summon millions of people from the earth. I am looking forward to that day, when those who have trusted in Jesus as their Savior will unite with Him in the air. Our earthly bodies will instantly change when we mortals will put on immortality and acquire bodies that will never be sick again and never die (Romans 8). It is my feeling that we will still be tangible beings capable of physical expression; in fact, we will be the same people we have always been. We will know each other and laugh together, so I'm very happy God has explained to us in the Bible that we will be free of homesickness, disease, pain and suffering. I really don't believe we will be floating spirits playing harps on puffy clouds. That image doesn't appeal to me at all. It is my belief that all those who have died before the rapture had different spiritual bodies and I can't honestly say what these bodies are like except I believe they are capable of singing, eating, dancing and are recognizable beings. After the rapture, their earthly bodies will resurrect no matter what condition their earthly remains are in. The Bible said the dead in Christ shall rise at the sound of the trumpet! It is my opinion that this is the new immortal bodies that will join the spiritual body in heaven and give everyone in heaven, at the time of the rapture, immortal physical bodies. Jesus, however, resurrected into the immortal physical body three days after his crucifixion. Only Jesus can do it. That is why it was so miraculously incredible because He didn't have only the spiritual body as others did when they died. He even asked his disciples to look at the scars in His hands and see that His body was indeed a physical body before he ascended to heaven.

God has given us an abundance of information to help us prepare for that glorious day. He also has told us that an event will occur and we will vanish in the "twinkling of an eye." When that happens, all earthly possessions will be left behind and we will receive our heavenly garments.

There is a beautiful song called "The Midnight Cry" sung by the Crabb Family. I get goose bumps every time I hear this song because my inner soul yearns for the coming of the Lord. Some of the lyrics are " When Jesus steps out on a cloud to call His children, the dead in Christ shall rise to meet Him in the air. And those that remain shall be quickly changed .At the midnight cry we'll be going home."

The mere fact that millions of people will vanish instantly in the rapture will cause great chaos here on earth for those left behind. People will instantly disappear before the eyes of others. All young children will vanish. This includes those still in the prenatal stage of development. Pregnant women will find that they are no longer carrying children in their wombs. All babies will disappear from hospital nurseries around the world. When we think of the scenario of what will happen when all these people disappear from the face of the earth we can imagine that airplane pilots will vanish and planes will crash. Drivers of automobiles will vanish, causing pile-ups on freeways. Houses will possible burn down when working stoves and candles are left unattended. Thousands of homes will be unoccupied with all household items left behind.

Many will recognize the truth of what has happened and some will be driven to suicide by the knowledge that they were left behind while their friends and family are now gone! The catastrophic impact of millions disappearing will cause so much grief and turmoil that people will sink into depression and desperately seek answers. They will look to their world leaders and the media for an explanation of what has just taken place around the globe. Questions will be asked such as these: Was it aliens? An environmental disaster? Religious cleansing? The rapture of the church?

I believe this is when the leaders will provide a scientific explanation in an attempt to appease the public. Some will surely voice their realization that it was the rapture of the church that took everyone to heaven. This explanation could be shot down, because those who are left behind will invoke the misguided claim that we all make it to heaven by being good people: "He's a good person! She's a good person! They are still here, so that explanation must be false!" Scripture tells us that it will be as it was during the days of Noah. Some will believe it was the evil ones who disappeared while the good ones remain.

Many will turn to Jesus during the first few days, doing whatever they can to enlighten anyone who will listen. There is hope. <u>You can still make heaven your eternal home</u>! Be aware of the spiritual warfare that will influence future events, because the tribulation period will start soon! And again, it will last for only seven years. As you read on, you will understand that life during this time will be extremely dangerous and difficult. But you'll also learn that most of the plagues that are predicted will affect only those who don't accept Jesus. Jesus will offer every opportunity for salvation to all people.

I want to take this opportunity to caution those who are reading this book during the tribulation period. If you are being tempted at this time to accept a numerical mark upon your forehead or your hand in allegiance to a leader, please go to chapter eight immediately. In the meantime, do not accept that mark upon your body. It is better to accept Jesus now, be martyred and go directly to heaven than to take the mark and be eternally damned by God.

When I say eternally, I mean ETERNALLY. Please heed these words.

All others are invited to read this book's remaining chapters in chronological order to gain an understanding of each phase of the tribulation as it unfolds.

Dear reader, these are not dreams or fables. They are infallible truths set forth in the Bible. Your unbelief will not change them. When Jesus returns in the rapture, only those who have accepted Him as their savior will be caught up in the clouds. Just like Enoch, who was not found because **God took him.**

2

The Anti-Christ

You've probably heard this term before. Growing up during the sixties, I heard a lot about the anti-Christ. For instance, my own father used to say that anyone who disagreed with him politically was either a Communist or the anti-Christ. All I knew at that time was that a powerful leader would persuade people to follow him instead of Jesus. He might even call himself Jesus to confuse people.

Now that I'm older and have studied scripture, I believe that a compelling leader will emerge during the tribulation period — when "all hell breaks loose." I suspect this person will be involved with satanic witchcraft and will have a seductive demeanor. He will radiate self-assurance, boldness, and the willingness to lead those who are distraught and grieving. He'll bring a false sense of peace to the world through deception and many will become his followers. He will be as a wolf in sheep's clothing, preying upon whomever he can devour. The anti-Christ is part of the satanic trinity, just as Christ is part of the Heavenly Trinity. The Heavenly Trinity is comprised of the Father, Son, and Holy Spirit. The counterfeit trio will include Satan, the anti-Christ, and the false prophet. This trio will imitate the holy trio.

The scripture uses many different names when referring to Satan. He is sometimes described as "the dragon" and is known as anti-God. He imitates the work of God the Father. Chapter twelve of Revelation calls Satan the devil and also "the dragon" when describing the vision of future events that John received from God. So when we read this book, we must realize that John is describing this vision in his own words. One such passage (Revelation 12:9) depicts the following scene: *The great dragon was hurled down — that ancient serpent called the devil, or Satan, who leads the whole world astray. He was hurled to the earth, and his angels with him.* This verse will be explained in more detail later. I've quoted it here to give you an idea of how many different names the Bible uses when discussing Satan.

In several places, the scripture refers to the anti-Christ as the beast. The anti-Christ imitates the work of God the Son. Verse 19:20 of Revelation tell us: *But the beast was captured, and with him the false prophet who had performed the miraculous signs on his behalf. With these signs he had deluded those who had received the mark of the beast and worshipped his image.*

The false prophet is sometimes called the second beast. He imitates the work of God the Holy Spirit. Verse 13:11 of Revelation says: *Then I saw another beast coming out of the earth. He had two horns like a lamb but he spoke like a dragon. He exercised all the authority of the first beast, whose fatal wound had been healed.*

The term "anti-Christ" means an enemy of Christ or one who usurps Christ's name and authority. Verses 2:3-4 of Thessalonians refers to the anti-Christ in the following passage:

Don't let anyone deceive you in any way, for that day will not come until the rebellion occurs and the man of lawlessness [or man of sin] is revealed, the man doomed to destruction. He will oppose and will exalt himself over everything that is called God or is wor-

shipped, so that he sets himself up in God's temple, proclaiming himself to be God.

He will be skilled at trickery and do wonderful things for those who believe he is the answer to their problems. Apostle Paul calls him the man of sin and tells us he will proclaim himself to be God during the great tribulation: *And then the lawless one [the anti-Christ] will be revealed, whom the Lord Jesus will overthrow with the breath of his mouth... The coming of the lawless one will be in accordance with the work of Satan displayed in all kinds of counterfeit miracles, signs and wonders...* (II Thessalonians 2:8-9)

The false prophet will serve as his spokesperson, continually bidding praise for his leader. Revelation 13:14-15 describes the deception inherent in his miracles: *Because of the signs he was given power to do on behalf of the first beast, he deceived the inhabitants of the earth. He ordered them to set up an image in honor of the beast that was wounded by the sword and yet lived. He was given power to give breath to the image of the first beast, so that it could speak and cause all who refused to worship the image to be killed.*

What does this mean? I take these verses literally. After the anti-Christ is wounded to the extent that many believe him to be dead, he will then simulate the resurrection of Jesus Christ and deceive many by acting as if he were raised from the dead. When this happens, the false prophet will erect a large statue of the anti-Christ; a statue that will actually be given a voice to simulate speech. Many will believe the anti-Christ to be the messiah.

Together the anti-Christ and the false prophet will do some amazing tricks for the public. But they will never be able to out-perform God. As hard as they might try, they will not be able to control or stop the plagues which God will unleash his forces in order to bring people to their knees; for only God can allow and control these events. The anti-Christ will not be able to cease the waters turning to blood, the unyielding darkness that will engulf parts of the earth, and the boils and horrendous sores that torment those who have taken the mark of the beast. His army will be dysfunctional and powerless against the army of God. All the ugly demonic creatures loosed upon the earth will be from Satan's realm. God will allow Satan and his demons to wreak tremendous havoc during this period.

There may be many prominent leaders during this time. How will you know for certain whom the anti-Christ is? It is prophesied that the anti-Christ will sign a seven-year peace treaty with Israel. The seven-year tribulation period will begin on the date the peace treaty is signed, and the treaty will be honored for the first 3½ years. Daniel 9:25–26 tells us: *Know and understand this: From the issuing of the decree to restore and rebuild Jerusalem until the Anointed One, the ruler, comes, there will be seven 'sevens' and sixty-two 'sevens.'[1] It will be rebuilt with streets and a trench, but in times of trouble. After sixty-two 'sevens,' the Anointed One will be cut off and will have nothing.* Verse 27 goes on to say: *....he will set up an abomination that causes desolation, until the end that is decreed is poured out on him.* Be alert and watch the world as this prophecy comes to pass.

Satan will use this leader as a pawn to bring the world to a place where he can exert the most control

---

[1] Weeks

over its media and its leaders. In Daniel 11:36-45, we receive more details about the anti-Christ.

In these verses, he is described as a king, for that will be the status the anti-Christ will attain among his followers: *The king will do as he pleases. He will exalt and magnify himself above every god and will say unheard-of things against the God of gods. He will be successful until the time of wrath is completed, for what has been determined must take place. He will show no regard for the gods of his fathers or for the one desired by women, nor will he regard any god, but will exalt himself above them all.* These verses reveal that he will magnify himself above everything, blaspheming the true God. He will be a secularist and brutal conqueror with confidence in his great military strength.

Revelation 13:3-8 states that: *One of the heads of the beast seemed to have had a fatal wound, but the fatal wound had been healed. The whole world was astonished and followed the beast. Men worshipped the dragon because he had given authority to the beast and asked, "Who is like the beast? Who can make war against him?"* This passage indicates that the beast dies (or that he appears to have died) before coming back to life. It also reveals that the whole world will be told, likely by the media, that he died and came back to life. The public will worship Satan for the power he bestows upon the anti-Christ.

Once the beast has apparently been resurrected from death, he will be worshipped by thousands who believe he is God. Revelation 13:5 states: *The beast was given a mouth to utter proud words and blasphemies and to exercise his authority for forty-two months.* And in verse 7, we read: *He was given power to make war against the saints and to conquer them. And he was given authority over every tribe, people, language and nation. All inhabitants of the earth will worship the beast — all whose names have not been written in the book of life belonging to the Lamb that was slain from the creation of the world.*

Our Heavenly Father, the one true God, is the one who will allow this to happen. Satan would have no power or authority without God's consent.

He will seek to destroy, but God will end his reign at the end of the tribulation. His days are numbered. At the conclusion of the Battle of Armageddon, the anti-Christ and the false prophet will be thrown into the lake of fire. Satan will join them after a thousand years. There they will be tormented, day and night, forever and ever.

3

Israel Is Attacked

Ezekiel 39:1-8: *1. Son of man, prophesy against Gog and say: This is what the Sovereign LORD says: I am against you, O Gog, chief prince of Meshech and Tubal. 2. I will turn you around and drag you along. I will bring you from the far north and send you against the mountains of Israel. 3. Then I will strike your bow from your left hand and make your arrows drop from your right hand. 4. On the mountains of Israel you will fall, you and all your troops and the nations with you. I will give you as food to all kinds of carrion birds and to the wild animals. 5. You will fall in the open field, for I have spoken, declares the Sovereign LORD. 6. I will send fire on Magog and on those who live in safety in the coastlands, and they will know that I am the LORD. 7. I will make known my holy name among my people Israel. I will no longer let my holy name be profaned, and the nations will know that I the LORD am the Holy One in Israel. 8. It is coming! It will surely take place, declares the Sovereign LORD. This is the day I have spoken of.*

Many scholars who have studied the Bible believe that Russia is "Gog." I can't state definitively that Gog is Russia because the Bible doesn't say so, but I believe it is possible. What the Bible does tell us is that a northern army of nations will lead their forces into Israel against the defenseless Jews; kindling God's wrath. God warned men against mistreating His people when through His prophet, Zechariah, He said: *For he that touches you [the Jew] touches the apple of His eye* (Zechariah 2:8).

If, on a map, you were to draw a straight line from Jerusalem to the North Pole, you will find that this line passes through the territory just beside Moscow. Moscow and Jerusalem are located near the same meridian, Jerusalem being at 35 degrees 10' and Moscow at 37 degrees 40' east of Greenwich. The northern armies could include Russian troops; in any event, they will be defeated when they invade Israel during the Last Days.

If you look back in history, you will see that whenever a nation has risen against Israel, God has avenged His people. While God is a God of love, He is also a God of vengeance and expresses righteous indignation every day. Psalm 7:11 tells us: *God judgeth the righteous, and God is angry with the wicked every day.*

The invasion of Israel will come after the peace treaty brokered by the anti-Christ has already been signed and the Israelis feel they are safe and secure. The nations likely to take part in the coalition invading Israel appear to be Turkey, Germany, Iran, and the other Arab states. This attack may come to pass because the Federated States of Europe will support the Jewish claims to Israel and guarantee their rights in the land of Palestine. The Arab states may turn to Russia for help in regaining their land.

It looks as though the western nations will not intervene (beyond merely voicing a diplomatic protest) for fear of escalating the war. I believe that Russia will want the land and that the anti-Christ will support her effort to seize it. The vast mineral deposits in the Dead Sea would provide enough potash to supply the needs of the entire world for 2000 years. Potash is used as fertilizer and a famine-filled world would covet its life-sustaining properties. But it also has another important application as a component of explosives. The value of potash, bromine and other chemical salts in the Dead Sea is currently estimated at $1,270,000,000,000.

Many believe that the end-time invasion of Israel by Russia and her allies will occur about midway through the tribulation period. This is when God will wipe out the attackers and protect Israel from harm. Many people of Israel and other nations of the world – upon seeing the miraculous power of Christ in the destruction of these attackers — will acknowledge Jesus Christ as their Lord and Savior. Ezekiel 38:23 says: *Thus I will manifest My greatness and My holiness and make Myself known in the eyes of many nations; they will know that I am the Lord.*

The great northern armies will falter and be destroyed. Israel will be protected and not one person of that nation will be killed or injured during the attack.

4

Tribulation Begins

After the rapture, thousands will flock to churches in their search for answers, peace, and guidance. The world will cry for peace and thousands will cling to the government's promises of relief. The anti-Christ will surface and, amidst wars and international crisis, he will bring world leaders together to draw up a special peace treaty with Israel promising protection that will last seven years. The scripture I'll share with you is from the New International Version of the Bible. The first scripture we will consider here is from the book of Daniel:

Daniel 9:27: *He will confirm a covenant with many for one 'seven.'[2] In the middle of the 'seven'[3] he will put an end to sacrifice and offering. And on a wing of the temple, he will set up an abomination that causes desolation,[4] until the end that is decreed is poured out on him.*

This means that the anti-Christ will put a covenant into effect for one week. During this week, the pagans will be offering animals and other sacrifices in the Temple that

---

[2] Week
[3] Week
[4] Matthew 24:15 and Mark 13:14 reference the prophet Daniel by speaking of an "abomination that causes desolation." This seems to refer both to Seleucid Emperor Antiochus Epiphanes IV, who sacrificed a pig on the altar of the Temple in Jerusalem in 167 B.C., as well as to a future abomination to be committed by the anti-Christ halfway through the tribulation. The scripture is not specific about what this abomination will be; it may be another sacrifice of a pig, or a human sacrifice, or yet some other atrocity.

will be rebuilt in Jerusalem. In the middle of the week, these sacrifices and offerings will come to an end. To understand the tradition of sacrifices, we have to be aware that during the period depicted in the Old Testament, God's forgiveness of sin was granted to people only when they sacrificed their most prized animals on an altar to Him. The chosen animals were usually lambs or calves because that is what most people used for trade. Their best animals were the most valuable for trade, so slaughtering them was a true sacrifice and God would recognize it as penance for sin. Sometimes people brought animals to the altar with the hope of gaining the Lord's favor or as a way of expressing gratitude to Him. Therefore, God gets angry when people offer sacrifices to pagan gods. When Jesus died on the cross, He became the ultimate sacrifice for our sins, ending the need for burnt offerings to God. That is why we call Jesus the "Lamb of God."

The Temple in Jerusalem will be built again. It will be erected for worship of the anti-Christ, not God. The original Temple in Jerusalem was built in 722 B.C., but it was later destroyed by the Babylonian army led by King Nebuchadnezzar in 586 B.C. Seventy years later, it was decreed that the city and the Temple would be rebuilt. The new Temple, built under the direction of Zerubbabel and Joshua, was called "Herod's Temple" (as it was renovated by Herod the Great), but in 70 A.D., the Romans (under the command of General Titus) defiled and destroyed it. The Temple was built to be a house of God — a divine dwelling in which all who accepted the Law of Moses could approach Him. It was to be a wall dividing Jews from pagans.

Over the course of four centuries, the Temple was repaired several times. It is prophesied that a new

Temple will be built on top of Mt. Moriah; the location where Abraham was to sacrifice Isaac. In the Muslims' distorted version of this story, Abraham brought Ishmael — not Isaac — to sacrifice. The Dome of the Rock Mosque and the Al-Aqsa Mosque currently occupy the Temple Mount. The book of Revelation prophesies that the anti-Christ will take over the Temple in Jerusalem and defile it, causing a great upheaval in the Jewish community.

I am amazed that this prophecy was written thousands of years ago when I consider the fact that, as I am writing this book, there is such turmoil between the Muslims and the Israelis. While the enmity began with Ishmael and Isaac, we are facing the prospect of mass destruction during a war in which many nations are involved. What a momentous event it will be when a peace treaty is drawn up between an international alliance (or perhaps an organization like the UN) and Israel! The world will surely participate in a huge celebration! I imagine that few will suspect the signing of this peace treaty will signal the beginning of the tribulation.

The beginning of the first 3½ years following this treaty should be a time of preparation for survival. I suggest finding a good sturdy structure to serve as a hideout in a rural area away from people. It should be strong enough to withstand a huge earthquake, and have two entrances in case one becomes impassable. Supplies should include non-perishable food, bottled water, sleeping bags, and medical supplies such as antibiotics, hygiene products, etc. You might find an abandoned home with a good basement. There will undoubtedly be many homes to choose from after millions have vanished in the rapture and thousands have been killed during the chaotic aftermath. It is important to prepare yourself for the kind of catastrophe that the world has never before experienced. Seven years may sound like a short period of time, but it will be so cataclysmic that it will seem to last forever.

During the first 3½ years, God will bring forth an army of 144,000 people.[5] When God mentioned this number, He was referring to a group of people LEFT on earth AFTER the rapture, a group that will evangelize the world. Let's look at Revelation 7:1-4: *After this I saw four angels standing at the four corners of the earth, holding back the four winds of the earth to prevent any wind from blowing on the land or on the sea or on any tree. **2.** Then I saw another angel coming up from the east, having the seal of the living God. He called out in a loud voice to the four angels who had been given power to harm the land and the sea: **3.** "Do not harm the land or the sea or the trees until we put a seal on the foreheads of the servants of our God." **4.** Then I heard the number of those who were sealed: 144,000 from **all the tribes of Israel.***

These people will be Jews who were still waiting for the true messiah when the rapture took place, and were thus left behind. But through a wonderful supernatural

---

[5] Many have been confused about the identity of these people. Some have based their faith on the idea that only 144,000 will be allowed into heaven and the only way they can become one of the appointed few is by doing good works. Unfortunately, those who have reached this conclusion failed to read the Bible carefully, as 144,000 does not reflect the number of people who will be admitted into heaven.

gift from God, and by way of the testimony of two witnesses, these tribe leaders learn and accept that the true messiah is none other than Jesus Christ, our Lord and Savior. Their lives are changed and they dedicate themselves to spreading the gospel throughout the world. The Lord will prepare their way in a supernatural exercise of divine power.

The verses in Revelation 7:1-4 suggest that before the world is beset by the plagues and disasters that bring on the sixth seal judgment at the end of the first quarter of the tribulation, God will raise up an army of 144,000 Jews who will come to Christ and evangelize the world. There will not be one Gentile among the 144,000.

Twelve thousand from each of the original twelve tribes will gather from all over the earth to form the 144,000. Revelation 7 states that the 144,000 sealed[6] are from the **tribes of Israel.** Twelve thousand from each of the tribes represent the total number.

Revelation 7:5-8 lists these tribes as the following:

5. From the tribe of Judah 12,000 were sealed,
   from the tribe of Reuben 12,000,
   from the tribe of Gad 12,000,
6. from the tribe of Asher 12,000,
   from the tribe of Naphtali 12,000,
   from the tribe of Manasseh 12,000,
7. from the tribe of Simeon 12,000,
   from the tribe of Levi 12,000,
   from the tribe of Issachar 12,000,

---

[6] What will be the nature of this seal? We do not know with certainty, but some believe perhaps it will be a number such as 777, and perhaps the anti-Christ will mark his own followers with 666. This is only a guess, however. The seal may be something else.

8. *from the tribe of Zebulun 12,000,*
from the tribe of Joseph 12,000,
from the tribe of Benjamin 12,000.

Matthew 24:14 says: *And this gospel of the kingdom will be preached in all the world as a witness to all the nations, and then the end will come.* I believe that during this time, more people will come to Christ than during any other period in history. Their preaching will be powerful and spread easily by way of the media and personal evangelism.

Who are the forefathers of these tribes?

They are all descendants of Abraham. Abraham had two sons; Ishmael was the son he had with Hagar, and Isaac was the son from Sarah. Isaac was born to Abraham and Sarah when they were well beyond their childbearing years, and his birth was considered a miracle from God. His descendants constitute the twelve tribes, to which I will devote more attention in chapter 14.

Isaac's twin sons were Esau and Jacob. Jacob's name was changed to Israel, which is why his descendants are known as Israelites. He had twelve sons: Reuben, Simeon, Levi, Judah, Zebulun, Issachar, Dan, Gad, Asher, Naphtali, Joseph and Benjamin. All of these sons, with the exception of Dan, yielded the tribes of Israel. (Joseph's son, Manasseh, yielded the twelfth tribe.)

Of course, there will be others outside of this group who will also evangelize for Jesus. People of all races and nationalities who have chosen to serve Jesus Christ will join together to spread the gospel to anyone who will listen. They will be putting their lives in danger by doing so, but they will do so regardless — for they will know the truth and will want to help as many people as possible before it is too late. However, the 144,000 Jews who will evangelize throughout the world will be protected by God and will not be martyred.

Revelation 7:2-3 lets us know that there will be a supernatural marking from God on the foreheads of His servants: *And I saw another angel coming from the east, carrying the Great Seal of the Living God. And he shouted out to those four angels who had been given power to injure earth and sea: "Hurt neither earth nor sea nor trees until we have placed the Seal of God upon the foreheads of His servants."*

Since there will be many "servants" of God, there is some confusion about who will bear this special mark. Some believe it is only for the 144,000 Jews and others believe the seal will be given to all believers. Only time will reveal the answer to this question.

Do not confuse this seal with the mark of the beast, which the anti-Christ will put on the hands or foreheads of unbelievers. The seal described in verse 7 of Revelation will be the mark of God and will identify <u>God's people</u> during the tribulation.

5

Two Witnesses

Revelation 11:3: *"And I will give power to my two witnesses, and they will prophesy for 1260 days, clothed in sackcloth."*

As I mentioned earlier, these two witnesses will be figures from the past. Many believe they will be Elijah and Moses, two very influential men in Jewish history who were known for performing miracles.

In Revelation 11:5, we read: *If anyone tries to harm them, fire comes from their mouths and devours their enemies. This is how anyone who wants to harm them must die. These men have power to shut up the sky so that it will not rain during the time they are prophesying.*

I believe they will do just that: cause a cessation of rain as they exhort the Jews to repent. This will cause a great famine in the land. They will incur much ridicule and hostility by identifying Jesus Christ as the messiah in a nation certain to consider this blasphemy against God. Lawmakers and those pledging allegiance to the anti-Christ will attempt to silence and destroy them. But the two witnesses will possess supernatural powers, including the ability to spew fire from their mouths and incinerate whoever rises against them. They will also have the power to turn water into blood and inflict plagues upon the earth. They will use whatever means are necessary to change the minds of those who have resolved to take on the mark of the beast as well as those who are still undecided. They will deliver a clear, bold and direct message with the hope that all who hear will understand and be moved to make the right decision.

Many will react with anger and die trying to stop the witnesses' ministry. Others will ridicule them, but keep a safe distance lest they meet the same fate as those who were incinerated.

Many will come to their knees, however, and decide to follow Christ. In doing so, they will be putting themselves in danger of being martyred. But this decision will also bring them peace of mind and strength of purpose if that is to be their destiny. These will be hard times. People will see their loved ones murdered, possibly by the guillotine, for choosing Christ.

Revelation 11:7 goes on to tell us: *And when they have finished their testimony, the beast that comes out of the abyss will make war with them, and overcome them and kill them.* The witnesses' time on earth will end after 1,260 days. The "beast that comes out of the abyss" is a reference to the anti-Christ. The anti-Christ will make war with the witnesses at the end of their days and ultimately murder them. While we don't know why God will allow this to happen, we are told that a miracle will follow. Their bodies will lie in the street of the great city — figuratively called Sodom and Egypt — where their Lord was crucified. For three-and-a-half days, men from every tribe, language and nation will gaze on the bodies and refuse them burial. It is likely that their corpses will be abused. Revelation 11:6-13 tells us: *They have the power to shut up the sky and keep the rain from falling during the days when they are speaking God's Word and the power over waters to turn them into blood, and to smite the earth with every plague, as often as they desire. (7)*

And when they have finished their testimony, the beast that comes up out of the abyss will make war with them and overcome them and kill them. (8) And their dead bodies will lie in the street of the great city, which mystically is called Sodom and Egypt, where also their Lord was crucified. (9) And those from the peoples and tribes and tongues and nations will look at their dead bodies for three days and a half, and will not permit their dead bodies to be laid in a tomb. (10) And those who dwell on the earth will rejoice over them and make merry; and they will send gifts to one another, because these two prophets tormented those who dwell on the earth. (11) And after the three days and a half the breath of life from God came into them (12) and they heard a loud voice from heaven saying, "Come up here." And they went up to heaven in the cloud and their enemies beheld them. (13) And in that hour there was a great earthquake, and the rest were terrified and gave glory to the God of heaven.

These verses reveal that people will gloat over the witnesses' dead bodies and celebrate their deaths, because they will believe these men were evil and the source of much agony. My interpretation is that, with the death of these witnesses, the people will believe their troubles are over and life is going to be good again. But when the two messengers suddenly rise to their feet, I can just imagine the shock of those who have spat upon, kicked, and abused their bodies. I'm sure the corpses will look wretched after three and a half days of abuse in the hot sun; but suddenly, they will rise! I believe everyone will hear them being summoned to heaven and witness their ascent. I think many will be affected by this miraculous sight, even to the point of falling on their knees and confessing their sins to God.

At this very hour, a severe earthquake will be unleashed and a tenth of the city will collapse. Seven thousand people will be killed in this earthquake, while survivors will be terrified and give glory to God. The Bible tells us that the seventh trumpet judgment and the third woe will follow this earthquake.

Wake Up Call

1st TRUMPET	2ND TRUMPET	3RD TRUMPET	4TH TRUMPET	5TH TRUMPET	6TH TRUMPET	INTERVAL	7TH TRUMPET
HAIL FIRE	FALLING METEOR BLOOD	STARS FALL FROM THE SKY	SUN, MOON, STARS	LOCUSTS ATTACK	SATAN'S ARMY	CHRIST TAKES CONTROL OF EARTH	EARTHQUAKE
1/3 Earth on Fire 1/3 Trees burned All Grass burned	1/3 ships, Fish destroyed 1/3 sea filled with blood	Poisons 1/3 of all water on Earth	1/3 of Sun, Moon & Stars Darkened	5 months of torture by scorpion stings	200 million warriors kill 1/2 of mankind	Two witnesses testify of Christ's coming	7000 die in Jerusalem People run to mountains
Revelation 8.7	Revelation 8.8–9	Revelation 8.10	Revelation 8.12	Revelation 9.1	Revelation 9.13	Revelation 11	Revelation 11.15

6

The Trumpet Judgments

We will see God unleash seven consecutive sets of judgments in each of three categories: the trumpet judgments, the seal judgments, and the bowl judgments. Each judgment upon the earth will be worse than the one before. The seven trumpet judgments will take place midway through the second half of the tribulation. The seal and the bowl judgments will occur near the end of this period. The trumpet judgments each begin with an angel sounding a trumpet — hence the name "trumpets judgments." Revelation 8:6 says: *Then the seven angels who had the seven trumpets prepared to sound them.*

The first of the trumpet judgments will bring hail, fire, and blood. Revelation 8:7 says: *And there came hail and fire mixed with blood, and it was hurled down upon the earth. A third of the earth was burned up, a third of the trees were burned up, and all the green grass was burned up.* In Joel 2:30, the prophet Joel says: *God will show wonders in the heavens and in the earth: blood and fire and pillars of smoke.*

Upon the sounding of the second trumpet, a great mountain burning with fire will be thrown into the sea. Revelation 8:8-9 states: *One third of the water will turn to blood. One third of creatures will die and one third of ships will sink.*

According to Revelation 8:10, a third angel will sound the trumpet and a great star named "Wormwood" will fall from the sky and cause rivers and springs to become bitter and poisonous.

Revelation 8:12 tells us that when the fourth angel sounds the trumpet, one-third of the moon, sun, and the stars will darken and never again be as bright as they once were.

Although these judgments sound bleak; let me remind you that God is on the throne and will bring victory to us. We must use this time to bring as many people to Christ as we can. Joel 2:31-32 says that: *The sun will be turned to darkness and the moon to blood before the coming of the great and dreadful day of the Lord. And everyone who calls on the name of the Lord will be saved.* This is a wonderful passage of scripture that offers hope to all who call upon Him.

The fifth trumpet of judgment brings the locusts of Apollyon. Revelation tells us an angel unlocks a bottomless pit, releasing smoke and locusts with scorpion-like stings that will torment unbelievers for five months. John says, *"In those days men will seek death and will not find it; they will want to die and death will flee them."* Clearly, the scorpions' sting will not be fatal, but so painful that many will unsuccessfully attempt to take their own lives. I will include all of the text here so you can read the scripture in its entirety:

Revelation 9*: 1. The fifth angel sounded his trumpet, and I saw a star that had fallen from the sky to the earth. The star was given the key to the shaft of the Abyss. 2. When he opened the Abyss, smoke rose from it like the smoke from a gigantic furnace. The sun and sky were darkened by the smoke from the Abyss. 3. And out of the smoke, locusts came down upon the earth and were given power like that of scorpions of the earth. 4. They were told not to harm the grass of the earth or any plant or tree, but only those people who did not have the seal* *of God on their foreheads. 5. They were not given power to kill them, but only to torture them for five months. And the agony they suffered was like that of the sting of a scorpion when it strikes a man. 6. During those days men will seek death, but will not find it; they will long to die, but death will elude them. 7. The locusts looked like horses prepared for battle. On their heads they wore something like crowns of gold, and their faces resembled human faces. 8. Their hair was like women's hair and their teeth were like lions' teeth. 9. They had breastplates like breastplates of iron and the sound of their wings was like the thundering of many horses and chariots rushing into battle. 10. They had tails and stings like scorpions, and in their tails they had power to torment people for five months. 11. They had as king over them the angel of the Abyss, whose name in Hebrew is Abaddon, and in Greek, Apollyon. 12. The first woe is past; two other woes are yet to come.*

As we have seen, Revelation 9:7 describes the locusts as resembling horses prepared for battle. On their heads are something like crowns of gold, and their faces resemble those of humans. Their hair is like women's hair and their teeth are like lions' teeth. I interpret these verses literally and believe that hideous creatures capable of inflicting a very painful sting will emerge from a bottomless pit.

Revelation 9:13-16 tells us that the sixth trumpet will release four angels: *It said to the sixth angel who had the trumpet, "Release the four angels who are bound at the great river Euphrates." And the four angels who had been kept ready for this very hour and day and month and year were released to kill a third of mankind. The number of the mounted troops was two hundred million. I heard their number.*

The angels mentioned here lead an army of 200 million demonic horsemen. As we continue in Revelation 9:17, we read:

17. The horses and riders I saw in my vision looked like this: Their breastplates were fiery red, dark blue, and yellow as sulfur. The heads of the horses resembled the heads of lions, and out of their mouths came fire, smoke and sulfur. 18. A third of mankind was killed by the three plagues of fire, smoke and sulfur that came out of their mouths. 19. The power of the horses was in their mouths and in their tails, for their tails were like snakes, having heads with which they inflict injury. 20. The rest of mankind that were not killed by these plagues still did not repent of the work of their hands; they did not stop worshipping demons, and idols of gold, silver, bronze, stone and wood—idols that cannot see or hear or walk. 21. Nor did they repent of their murders, their magic arts, their sexual immorality or their thefts.

These verses describe the horses as having heads resembling the heads of lions. A third of mankind will be killed by the three plagues of fire, smoke and sulfur that come out of their mouths. Their tails will be similar to snakes, having heads that inflict injury. The Bible goes on to tell us that the rest of mankind will still not repent. They will continue worshipping demons and idols. They will continue their murders, magic arts, sexual immorality and thefts.

The third woe will be announced by the sound of the seventh trumpet. This one introduces a series of divine judgments. Here I will provide, in their entirety, verses 11: 15-19 of Revelation:

15. The seventh angel sounded his trumpet, and there were loud voices in heaven, which said: "The kingdom of the world has become the kingdom of our Lord and of his Christ, and he will reign forever and ever." ***16.*** *And the twenty-four elders, who were seated on their thrones before God, fell on their faces and worshipped God,* ***17.*** *saying:*

"We give thanks to you, Lord God Almighty, the One who is and who was, because you have taken your great power and have begun to reign.

18. *The nations were angry; and your wrath has come. The time has come for judging the dead, and for rewarding your servants the prophets and your saints and those who reverence your name, both small and great— and for destroying those who destroy the earth."*

19. *Then God's temple in heaven was opened, and within his temple was seen the ark of his covenant. And there came flashes of lightning, rumblings, peals of thunder, an earthquake and a great hailstorm.*

It would be an understatement to say that the creatures mentioned above will be hideous. These judgments will inflict pain and horror upon the people who harden their hearts against God and the truth. Because their hearts will not be open to accepting the true God, they will be filled with bitterness and anger. Unfortunately, their choices will make their lives more miserable. This situation reminds me of a story about a stubborn child. This child was told not to wade into a creek because the water was too cold. He didn't believe the water was too cold and was angry at his father for forbidding him to play in the creek. When the father turned his back, the child rebelliously waded into the cold creek to play. Before long, the child was miserably chilled and very unhappy. His father punished him for disobeying, but gave him dry clothes along with a warning to obey in the future. The child didn't heed his father's warning. The next day, he went back into the cold water and drowned.

God, our heavenly Father, warns us again and again. But we stubbornly ignore His warnings and get punished for our disobedience. Some of us will die because we will reject His love and continually venture where we shouldn't. We can't blame God for our stubbornness.

Wake Up Call

1st SEAL	2ND SEAL	3RD SEAL	4TH SEAL	5TH SEAL	6TH SEAL	7TH SEAL
White Horse and Rider	Red Horse and Rider	Black Horse and Rider	Pale Horse and Rider	Altar	Great Earthquake	Silence and Fire
Signifies Anti-Christ and warfare	Signifying War Bloodshed	Signifying Famine and Disease	Signifying Death and Hades	Souls of Martyrs wearing white robes	Sun turns black Moon turns red Stars fall to earth	Silence for 30 minutes Angel hurls fire to earth Thunder Lightning Earthquake
Revelation 6.1-2	Revelation 6.3-4	Revelation 6.5-6	Revelation 6.7-8	Revelation 6.9-11	Revelation 6.12-17	Revelation 8.1-5

7

Seal Judgments

*I*t will be helpful to review a bit of history before considering the "seal" judgments. The Book of Revelation refers to the Hebrew practice of unveiling a scroll by unrolling it to read the text.

In ancient tradition, continued by Jews today, a scroll was covered by a cloth or veil. To read the scroll, it first had to be unveiled. The scroll was often sealed many times and in many places with hot wax. Each seal had to be broken before the scroll could be unrolled any further. In the fifth chapter of Revelation, we find Christ seated on the throne, holding a scroll in His hands. John, who wrote the Book of Revelation, tells of watching Jesus open the seven-sealed book (scroll): *Then I saw in the right hand of Him who sat on the throne a scroll with writing on both sides and sealed with seven seals...*

The seven seals discussed in Revelation are a direct reference to this scroll that Jesus holds which will be opened and unsealed seven times; revealing and releasing each seal judgment one by one. After the signing of the treaty there will be eighteen months of peace. During this time global communication will be reestablished as world leaders unite and great multitudes of people come to Christ. After this respite it is expected that the seven seal judgments will immediately begin and continue throughout the first 3 ½ years of tribulation.

The temple of Jerusalem will be rebuilt. (This temple was originally built in 722 B.C. and later destroyed by the Babylonian Army in 586 B.C. During temple's history, it had been defiled, demolished and rebuilt again and again. It was to be a House of God; a divine dwelling where all humanity could approach God. (It was regarded as the wall dividing Jews from pagans.) This temple symbolizes God's blessing to His chosen people and is of great importance to have it rebuilt. What seems to be a great tribute to God and the opportunity to regain status will become a blasphemy to God when the anti-Christ purposely defiles it as a "slap in the face" to the Jewish people. When the seven seal judgments begin angels are standing before the throne of God awaiting instruction. Only God knows the day and the hour when the scroll is to be ceremoniously unveiled. In Revelation 5:7, we read:

He [Jesus] came and took the scroll from the right hand of Him [God] who sat on the throne. And when he had taken it, the four living creatures and twenty-four elders fell down before the Lamb. Each one had a harp and they were holding golden bowls full of incense, which are the prayers of the saints. And they sang a new song: "You are worthy to take the scroll and to open the seals, because you were slain, and with your blood you purchased men for God from every tribe and language and people and nation. You have made them to be a kingdom and priests to serve God, and they will reign on the earth.

In Revelation 6:1-2, John recounts: *"I watched as the Lamb[i] opened the first of seven seals. Then I heard one of the four living creatures say in a voice of thunder, "Come!" I looked, and there before me was a white horse! Its rider held a bow and he was given a crown, and he rode out as a conqueror bent on conquest."*

Thus we learn that the first seal reveals a white horse and rider, signifying the anti-Christ and his kingdom. The bow he carries is a symbol of warfare. He will wear a crown, which indicates that he is successful in his efforts.

Revelation 6:3-4 continues: *When the Lamb opened the second seal, I heard the second living creature say "Come!" Then another horse came out, a fiery red one. Its rider was given power to take peace from the earth and to make men slay each other. To him was given a large sword.*

Thus we learn that the second seal reveals a red horse, signifying war, possibly World War III. The ever-increasing stockpile of nuclear weapons in several countries has created the very real possibility of a third world war.

Revelation 6:5-6 continues: *When the Lamb opened the third seal, I heard the second living creature say, "Come!" I looked and there before me was a black horse! Its rider was holding a pair of scales in his hand. Then I heard what sounded like a voice among the four living creatures, saying, "A quart of wheat for a day's wages, and three quarts of barley for a day's wages, and do not damage the oil and the wine!"*

From this passage, we learn that the third seal reveals a black horse, signifying famine and disease. We can assume these will be caused by the war. We will likely see plagues that are already identified as a threat today, such as AIDS and other sexually transmitted diseases, malaria, cholera, dysentery, and new strains that are resistant to medication. One-fourth of the world's population will be wiped out during the second, third and fourth judgments.

In Revelation 6:7-8, John says: *When the Lamb opened the fourth seal, I heard the voice of the fourth living creature say, "Come!" I looked, and there before me was a pale horse! Its rider was named Death, and Hades was following close behind.*

This passage indicates that the fourth seal reveals a pale horse, symbolizing death. One quarter of the earth's population will die as a result of the war and its aftermath. But we should note that the verse says "Death and Hades followed with him." This means that only the non-believers will die. Because if the phrase was referring to believers, we know they would go not to Hades but to heaven. It is very important for you to realize that if you have chosen Jesus as your savior, you will be protected from this horseman.

During the subsequent three months, the fifth, sixth and seventh seals of judgment will be unleashed upon the earth. The fifth seal refers to the martyrdom of tribulation saints. In Revelation 6:9-11, John testifies: *When he opened the fifth seal, I saw under the altar the souls of those who had been slain because of the word of God and the testimony they had maintained. They called out in a loud voice, "How long, Sovereign Lord, holy and true, until you judge the inhabitants of the earth and avenge our blood?" Then each of them was given a white robe, and they were told to wait a little longer, until the number of their fellow servants and brothers who were to be killed as they had been was completed.*

My dear friends, these days will be extremely difficult. You will see death and destruction all around you. Surely you will want to be one of the tribulation saints who will live through the entire seven years and see the wonderful second coming of Christ! But it is highly possible that you or someone close to you will be martyred for the sake of Christ. The anti-Christ will seek to destroy you and will do whatever he must to complete that task. Most Christians will need to go into hiding and find underground shelter. Food will be scarce and Christians will need to pool their resources for survival. Don't give in to the promises of the world leaders. Their promises may offer you temporary comfort, but they will ultimately lead to your eternal destruction. As you read on, you will find that most of the plagues imposed upon the earth's population will only affect those who have not chosen Jesus Christ as their Savior and whose names are not written in the Lamb's Book of Life.

The sixth seal judgment will yield a great earthquake. In Revelation 6:12-17, John states: *I watched as he opened the sixth seal. There was a great earthquake. The sun turned black like sackcloth made of goat hair, the whole moon turned blood red, and the stars in the sky fell to the earth, as late figs drop from a fig tree when shaken by a strong wind. The sky receded like a scroll, rolling up, and every mountain and island was removed from its place.*

Thus we learn that the earth will suffer another earthquake, so massive that every mountain and island will be moved out of its place. It will sweep the entire earth and cause massive destruction. The greatest earthquake in history will initiate the seven trumpet seal judgments, which will unfold next. These will serve as final warnings from a loving God who does not want anyone to miss eternity in heaven. Day will turn into night and the moon will turn blood red. Meteors and fireballs will fall to the earth. In Revelation 8:1-2, John continues: *When he opened the seventh seal, there was silence in heaven for about half an hour.* He goes on to say in Revelations 8:5: *Then the angel took the censer, filled it with fire from the altar, and hurled it on the earth; and there came peals of thunder, rumblings, flashes of lightning and an earthquake.*

It will take twenty-one months for the seven seal judgments to unfold. What happens afterward will be worse than anything humankind has ever experienced. The first half of the tribulation will issue from the wrath of the anti-Christ. The second half of the tribulation will issue from the wrath of God.

Wake Up Call

1st VIAL	2ND VIAL	3RD VIAL	4TH VIAL	5TH VIAL	6TH VIAL	7TH VIAL
BOILS	SEA OF BLOOD	RIVERS OF BLOOD	OPPRESSIVE HEAT	DARKNESS	RIVER EUPHRATES DRIED UP	HAIL
Those who take the mark will be tormented by nasty sores	Everything living in the ocean dies	All rivers, springs, creeks turn to blood	Sun scorches all people on earth	Earth thrust into darkness	Army marches	Cities colapse
Revelation 16:2	Revelation 16:3	Revelation 16:4-7	Revelation16:8-9	Revelation 16:10-11	Revelation 16:12-16	Revelation 16:17-21

8

The Great Tribulation

The tribulation period will last for seven years, and although the first half will be easier than the second, it will still be filled with trials and disasters on the earth. The signing of the peace treaty with Israel might happen at any time; it could happen before the rapture, or after. Many believe that it will take place between three weeks and three months after the rapture. But no one really knows. Only God knows.

Earthquakes, famine, and storms will kill thousands of people. God's chosen people will begin to rebuild the temple.

Daniel was the first prophet to write about the anti-Christ's one-world government (Daniel 2:31-45). He predicted that during the last days, ten kings would form one final world government. But it will be the one-world religion that will bring the wrath of God down upon the earth. Revelation 17:6-18 speaks of the global church and of the abominations on the earth.

The second three-and-a-half years will be known as the great tribulation period. These days will be truly awful; Jesus said in Matthew 24:21-22 that: *Then there will be great tribulation, such as has not been since the beginning of the world until this time, no, nor ever shall be. And unless those days are shortened, no flesh would be saved; but for the elect's sake those days will be shortened.*

It will be an ugly time of lawlessness and immorality. Revelation 9:20-21 lists the top seven sins of the tribulation as: rebellion against God, worship of demons, idolatry, murder, sorcery, sexual immorality and theft. These sins are already rampant in our society today. Immorality pervades our television programs, movies, and even commercials. We have become complacent and accepting of this. It is already a challenge to monitor what our children are viewing. Because there is a little girl in our family, I have had to block access to certain television channels that were supposedly designed for children but are full of ungodly messages. Prime family-time TV is full of commercials promising sexual enhancement! It is just a matter of time before this will be the standard fare for all viewers at any time of day. All discretion will be gone.

The anti-Christ will defile the temple and set the great tribulation in motion. He will gain control of the world's money and use the power he acquired during the previous three years to impose a system known as "the mark of the beast" – so named because the anti-Christ is called "the beast" throughout the Bible. We already have the technology to bring such a system into effect. Computer chips are already being placed beneath the skin of humans as experimental devices. Satellites can not only pinpoint the location of those chips, but can take a photo of the person's driver's license if he is holding it in his hand. We are also becoming a cashless society. There is a reason for that! One day these chips will likely be embedded within everyone – chips bearing every aspect of an individual's personal, financial and medical history (information such as birth date, social security number, bank account information, family history, medical history, employment information, credit history, etc.).

No one will be able to engage in commerce without the beast's mark on his hand or forehead. It will be mandatory. However, all who accept this mark will be making a choice to worship the beast, to pledge allegiance to the anti-Christ and reject the preaching of the two witnesses.

By accepting the mark, you will be condemning yourself to eternal damnation. Revelation 14:9-12 warns that all who worship the beast and his image — and receive his mark on their foreheads or hands — shall suffer God's wrath. They will be cast into hell and tormented with fire and brimstone. Taking the mark is irreversible. You can't change your mind once you've done it!

Many Christians will be martyred for refusing the mark and withholding allegiance from the beast. But they will also immediately be in the presence of the Lord. I can't express in words how wonderful life will be in heaven. We will be more alive there than we have ever been on this earth — for the moment we were born in our earthly bodies, we began dying. But when we receive our heavenly immortal bodies, we will be truly alive — feeling, tasting, laughing, and enjoying life to the fullest! This is such an exciting idea!

In the meantime, after the mark is introduced, people will be encouraged to reject Biblical teachings and join the one-world church.

The next judgments are called the vial judgments (or bowl judgments) and they will wreak havoc upon those who have taken the mark of the beast. Those who have taken the mark will face the first vial judgment: a plague of foul and loathsome sores. No tribulation saint who has chosen Jesus as his or her savior will suffer (Revelation 16:2).

The second vial judgment is mentioned in Revelation 16:3 and talks of the sea turning into blood. This is a judgment against those who have sinned against God and turned their back on His word. The sea creatures will die and float to the surface; the stench and decay is sure to be overwhelming.

Revelation 16:4-7 tells us that the third vial judgment will cause all the water in rivers and springs to turn into blood. There will be no clean drinking water anywhere!

Revelation 16:8-9 tells us that with the fourth vial judgment, the sun will scorch men and they still will not turn from their wicked ways.

The fifth vial judgment will bring darkness upon the beast's kingdom (Revelation 16:10-11). This is a special judgment on the land or city where the anti-Christ dwells. These verses mention that during this time, people will still be afflicted with the sores from the first bowl judgment and the darkness will intensify their suffering. Verse 10 tells us: *And they gnawed their tongues because of the pain.* Verse 11 says: *They blasphemed God because of their pain and their sores and did not repent of their deeds.* It is possible that their hearts will be hardened against God, for they will have completely turned their backs on Him and doomed themselves eternally.

Two things will happen during the sixth vial judgment: first, the Euphrates River — the natural dividing line between the east and the west — will run dry in preparation for the armies of the kings from the east. Next, demonic forces will bring the armies of the world to the valley of Megiddo, where they will try in vain to oppose Jesus.

Finally, the seventh vial judgment will bring on the most massive and forceful earthquake the world has ever seen (Revelation 16:17-21). A voice from the heavens will cry out, "It is DONE." Huge hailstones — weighing over 100 pounds each – will fall to the earth. And this will usher in a battle unprecedented in scale and brutality: the Battle of Armageddon.

9

Your Decision

"We make our decisions and then our decisions make us"

—Frank Borham

The terms "saved" and "born-again" describe those who have accepted Christ as their personal savior. Born-again Christians are saved from the wrath of God against sinners, and from eternity in hell. They are assured of eternal life with Jesus Christ in Heaven. "Born-again" doesn't mean being born again physically, but spiritually.

Just as there are physical laws that govern the physical universe, so there are spiritual laws that govern your relationship with God. Consider the following passages:

Verily, verily, I say unto you, he that heareth my word, and believeth in Him that sent me, hath everlasting life, and shall not come into condemnation; but is passed from death unto life. (John 5:24)

For God so loved the world that whoever believeth in Him shall have everlasting life. (John 3:16)

All honor to God, the God and Father of our Lord Jesus Christ, for it is His boundless mercy that has given us the privilege of being born again, so that we are now members of God's own family. Now we live in hope of eternal life because Christ rose again from the dead. And God has reserved for His children the priceless gift of eternal life; it is kept in heaven for you, pure and undefiled, beyond reach of change and decay. (Peter 1:3-5)

And in John 10:10, Christ says: *I came that they might have life, and might have it abundantly.*

Man is sinful and separated from God. Romans 3:23 tells us: *All have sinned and fall short of the glory of God.* Man was created to have fellowship with God, but because of his own stubborn self-will, he chose to go his own way and his fellowship with God was broken. This self-will is characterized by pride, rebellion and sin. Jesus Christ offers the only redemption for man's sin. Through Him you can know and experience God's love and plan for your life.

God demonstrates His own love toward us, in that while we were yet sinners, Christ died for us. (Romans 5:8)

Jesus said to him, "I am the way, and the truth, and the life; no one comes to the Father but through me." (John 14:6)

God expects you to come as you are. You do not need to change your ways before coming to Him. Please come to Him now and allow Him to be with you and help you become the person you want to be. So many religions and so many people have done their best to complicate the simple message of Christ. You can't get to Heaven by your good works; Heaven is a gift from God. You must decide for yourself; no one can decide for you or attain Heaven for you by praying on your behalf. If you place your trust in Him, God will freely forgive you for your sins. He knows your heart and is not as concerned with your words as He is with the attitude of your heart.

If you would like to receive Christ as your Savior but are not sure how to do so, I suggest offering the following prayer or one like it:

Dear Heavenly Father,

I believe you sent your son, Jesus, to die on the cross for our sins. I believe He was raised from the dead and will soon come again for us. I admit I have sinned and I ask you to forgive my sins and cleanse me. I ask Jesus to be my Lord and savior and I will serve Him as long as I live. Amen.

With the offering of this simple prayer, you can be assured that God has heard you and accepted you into the Family of God. Your name will immediately be written in the Lamb's Book of Life. I don't know what circumstances you are experiencing as you say this prayer, or whether or not the rapture has yet taken place. If you are living during the tribulation period, by now you may very well have a heavenly mark on your forehead, given to you as a gift by God Himself. You may or may not be able to see it yourself, but I am sure it will be perceptible to other believers. I encourage you to find a church and seek out other believers in order to create the support network you all will need during the next few years.

Maybe you don't feel ready to make a decision, but there are only two choices. If you haven't chosen Jesus, you have chosen to follow Satan. I know this may sound harsh, but let me explain. Satan will do all he can to fill our minds with lies. These lies include the idea that you have plenty of time to make a choice and that you shouldn't let anyone push you into a decision. What he isn't telling you is that if you don't choose Jesus, you will belong to him — Satan the deceiver. He knows this but he doesn't want you to know it. Jesus Christ has purchased your opportunity for redemption by dying on the cross and shedding His blood to cleanse you of all sin.

At this point, you might be thinking, "But I go to church, or I've gone to church…I'm a good person." However, going to church doesn't make you a Christian, just as stepping into a mosque or synagogue wouldn't make you a Muslim or a Jew. You must make a conscious decision to follow Christ; otherwise, you are following Satan.

If you are still living in the days before the rapture of the church, please remember that God's word never changes and He does promise in John 6:37 that: *Him that cometh to me I will in no wise cast out.* This means that He loves you and accepts you and would never reject you.

Maybe you've been hurt or deceived; maybe you are grieving or suffering. We read in Romans 5:3-4 that: *Suffering produces perseverance; perseverance produces character; and character, hope.* For me, suffering can also be accompanied by emotional and physical weakness. After the death of my daughter, I tried to pray, but I was in shock and didn't know whether I could make it through the next hour, let alone another day. But after reading Romans 8:26-27, I understood that even though I couldn't speak, I could still maintain close communication with God.

The Spirit helps us in our weakness. We do not know what we ought to pray for, but the Spirit himself intercedes for us with groans that words cannot express. And he who searches our hearts knows the mind of the Spirit, because the Spirit intercedes for the saints in accordance with God's will. (Romans 8:26-27)

Please find a Bible that you can read. Start with the New Testament. There are many translations to choose from and you may not have any idea about which one to buy. I would recommend the NIV (New International Version) or The Message translation. These are very accessible translations that can help us understand the scripture.

Give frequent thanks to God that Christ is in your life and that He will never leave you.

Deuteronomy 31:6 tells us: *Be strong and courageous. Do not be afraid or terrified because of them, for the LORD your God goes with you; he will never leave you nor forsake you.*

You can be assured that Christ lives in you and that you will have eternal life from the very moment you invite Him into your heart. HE will not deceive you.

My main purpose for writing this book was not to scare anyone by relating the horrors to come during the tribulation period, but rather to offer you the knowledge that the Lord is with you and will never leave or forsake you. I wanted to provide understanding of the scripture's prophecy of the last days. This booklet was specifically written for those who have been left behind after the rapture, those who are seeking guidance and insight into what is happening and what is yet to come. God has filled the Bible with the prophecy of the last days so that we will know what to expect. Our precious heavenly Father loves us so much that He gave us the schedule of events in advance, so we can be prepared and secure in the knowledge that He is in control and HE WILL WIN. We already know the ending of the story and it is glorious! The thought of the Glorious Appearing gives me goose bumps. I envision the surviving tribulation saints looking up into the sky and seeing the clouds part. I can picture the Lord Jesus Christ riding on a great white horse, surrounded by angels and martyred saints. I imagine Him coming down from the sky in glorious splendor, and I know the beautiful music and angelic singing will be magnificent to hear. This is definitely an event to look forward to! But the best will still be yet to come, for after the millennium, we will be forever with the Lord.

10

Glorious Appearing

The Bible mentions Jesus coming to us three times. The first time was His birth in Bethlehem; the second will be when he comes for His church during the rapture (though people won't see Him when He comes). The third time, all eyes will be upon Him as He descends amidst the clouds during what the Bible calls the "second coming" (since it will be the second coming in the clouds) or the "Glorious Appearing." If you survive the seven years of tribulation, you will be rewarded with the sight of the "Glorious Appearing of Christ." Jesus will come back to earth to set up His Kingdom and rule over the earth for one thousand years, a segment of time called the millennium. Matthew: 24:29-31 says: *Immediately after the distress of those days the sun will be darkened, and the moon will not give its light; the stars will fall from the sky, and the heavenly bodies will be shaken! At that time the sign of the Son of Man will appear in the sky, and all the nations of the earth will mourn. They will see the Son of Man coming on the clouds of the sky, with power and great glory. And he will send his angels with a loud trumpet call, and they will gather his elect from four winds, from one end of the heavens to the other.*

This sounds to me as if everything will become so dark for a moment that you will not even be able to see your hand in front of your face. Have you ever been in darkness like that? I once toured the Oregon Caves and the guide led us down into a huge cavern filled with stalactites and stalagmites. In this cavern, he turned off his flashlight and we were instantly thrown into total darkness. Even though I was a child, this memory has always stayed with me, for I was totally blind. Then the guide lit a tiny match that illuminated the entire cavern.

This is the kind of darkness I envision when Jesus makes his very dramatic entrance. Many people will mourn because they didn't believe the truth and turned their backs on Him. What a moment of despair! They made the wrong choice and their evil path will lead to their demise. One comparison that comes to mind is a person who has decided to cheat on an exam. That person will rationalize his choice, telling himself that he deserves to pass the test, and the teacher is to blame for giving him so much homework that he didn't have time to study! Then when the teacher catches him cheating, the guilt and shame and shock of being caught brings him to despair. We can multiply these feelings a hundredfold for all those who will realize that Jesus has come and they have chosen the wrong path. This is why the verse says that all of the nations of the earth will mourn. Thousands of people will be devastated by the sight of Jesus coming in clouds of great glory. But there will also be many who'll be elated that the tribulation period is now over. I believe there will be much rejoicing and excitement.

I can just imagine the glory of seeing the clouds part and Jesus descending among a band of angels, with trumpets blaring and glorious heavenly singing audible to every living creature on the earth… it is sure to be awe-inspiring.

When Jesus returns to the earth, He will descend to the Mount of Olives and it will split in two. The fault beneath it will split the mountain wide open. As it says in Zechariah 14:3-5: *3. Then the LORD will go out and fight against those nations, as he fights in the day of battle. 4. On that day his feet will stand on the Mount of Olives, east of Jerusalem, and the Mount of Olives will be split in two from east to west, forming a great valley, with half of the mountain moving north and half moving south. 5. You will flee by my mountain valley, for it will extend to Azel. You will flee as you fled from the earthquake in the days of Uzziah king of Judah. Then the LORD my God will come and all the holy ones with him.*

In Revelation 19:6, we read: *Then I heard what sounded like a great multitude, like a roar of rushing waters and like loud peals of thunder, shouting: Hallelujah! For our Lord God Almighty reigns. Let us rejoice and be glad and give him glory!*

What a time of celebration for all those who have been separated from family and friends. They will finally be reunited, knowing they will never be separated again. The saints from heaven who departed in the rapture and all Christians who died during the tribulation will reunite with the survivors still on earth.

Even though many will be rejoicing, God's judgment of the cowering evil leaders and marked followers will be imminent. Can you imagine someone who is entirely evil, without any redeeming features? Now imagine someone who is all good, without a trace of evil. Originally, Satan was a beautiful angel who was given leadership. He was called the morning star and he enjoyed the power he was given. He became self-centered and thought he could rise up against God and overpower Him. Isaiah 14:12 tells us that God became very disappointed in him and cast him out of heaven:

"How you have fallen from heaven, O morning star, son of dawn! You have been cast down to the earth, you who once laid low the nations! You said in your heart, 'I will ascend to heaven; I will raise my throne above the stars of God; I will sit enthroned on the mount of assembly, on the utmost heights of the sacred mountain. I will ascend above the tops of the clouds; I will make myself like the Most High.' But you are brought down to the grave, to the depths of the pit."

Ezekiel 28:12, 17 says: *Son of man, take up a lament concerning the king of Tyre and say to him: "This is what the Sovereign LORD says: 'You were the model of perfection, full of wisdom and perfect in beauty... ^{17.} Your heart became proud on account of your beauty, and you corrupted your wisdom because of your splendor. So I threw you to the earth; I made a spectacle of you before kings.'"*

We can also read about the angels who followed Satan to earth in Revelation 12:7-9: *And there was war in heaven. Michael and his angels fought against the dragon, and the dragon and his angels fought back but he was not strong enough, and they lost their place in heaven. The great dragon was hurled down — that ancient serpent called the devil, or Satan, who leads the whole world astray. He was hurled to the earth, and his angels with him.*

We have all heard of demons. The angels that were cast out of heaven for following Satan lost their beauty when they turned their back on God and His love. They became horrid evil creatures without any possibility of gaining favor with God. They are doomed to hell and torment and all aspects of sorcery and witchcraft are derived from demonic powers. Engaging in fortune telling or visiting a psychic can bring horrible consequences, as we learn in the following verses:

Deuteronomy 18:10-12,14 cautions us: *No one be found among you who sacrifices his son or daughter in the fire, who practices divination or sorcery, interprets omens, engages in witchcraft, [11] or casts spells, or who is a medium or spiritist or who consults the dead. [12] Anyone who does these things is detestable to the LORD, and because of these detestable practices the LORD your God will drive out those nations before you. [14] The nations you will dispossess listen to those who practice sorcery or divination. But as for you, the LORD your God has not permitted you to do so.*

Galatians 5:19-21 states: *So I say, live by the Spirit, and you will not gratify the desires of the sinful nature. [17] For the sinful nature desires what is contrary to the Spirit and the Spirit what is contrary to the sinful nature. They are in conflict with each other, so that you do not do what you want. [18] But if you are led by the Spirit, you are not under law.*

[19] The acts of the sinful nature are obvious: sexual immorality, impurity and debauchery; [20] idolatry and witchcraft; hatred, discord, jealousy, fits of rage, selfish ambition, dissensions, factions [21] and envy; drunkenness, orgies, and the like. I warn you, as I did before, that those who live like this will not inherit the kingdom of God.

And Mark 8:36 asks: *What good is it for a man to gain the whole world, yet forfeit his soul?*

We cannot initiate direct contact with good spirits. Many people join occult practices, thinking "*I will only contact good spirits.*" But God has prohibited us from initiating contact with the spirit world. Therefore, it follows that all good angels will obey His laws and not respond to our attempts to make direct contact. If we do attempt to make contact with the spirit world, it will be the evil spirits that take advantage of this and allow contact, while *claiming* to be good.

God **does** send angels to us in response to our prayers, but generally they do **not** make direct visible contact.

Now that we know a little more about Satan, we might wonder why he wants to destroy us. It's important to realize that he and his fallen angels once had everything in heaven. When they were cast out, they lost it all. All love, peace, contentment, and joy was taken away from them. Now they are purely evil beings who hate Christians because they know we will eventually dwell in heaven with our Lord and they will never again have that privilege. Their goal is to keep as many people as possible away from eternal life with Jesus. God, on the other hand, is LOVE. There is no evil in him. He is all goodness and can look only upon goodness. He can't look upon sin. That is why when Jesus was on the cross and all the sins of the world were put upon Him, God had to turn away. In Matthew 27:45,46, verses that discuss the death of Jesus, we are told: *From the sixth hour until the ninth hour darkness came over the land, and at the ninth hour Jesus cried out in a loud voice, "Eloi, Eloi lama sabachthani?" which means "My God, My God, why have you forsaken me?"*

At this moment, Jesus felt loneliness and a sense of separation from His father in heaven. This was part of the ordeal He endured as our Lamb of sacrifice, which did away with any future need for people to redeem their sins by making burnt offerings to the Lord.

To return to Revelation 19, the scripture discussing the Glorious Appearing of Jesus Christ, let's resume at the point where He has descended to earth on a white horse to judge the enemy. Revelation 19:11-15 tells us: *I saw heaven standing open and there before me was a white horse, whose rider is called Faithful and True. With justice he judges and makes war. His eyes are like blazing fire, and on his head are many crowns.* Verse 15 says: *He will rule with an iron scepter. He treads the winepress of the fury of the wrath of God Almighty. On his robe and on his thigh he has this name written: "KING OF KINGS AND LORD OF LORDS."*

The battle shall be fought against the enemy but I don't expect it will take very long. It may last for only one day, for the Bible immediately tells us that the beast was captured and thrown, along with the false prophet, into the lake of fire and burning sulfur. Revelation 19:19-21 tells us: *Then I saw the beast and the kings of the earth and their armies gathered together to make war against the rider on the horse and his army. But the beast was captured, and with him the false prophet who had performed the miraculous signs on his behalf. With these signs he had deluded those who had received the mark of the beast and worshipped his image. The two of them were thrown alive into the fiery lake of burning sulfur. The rest of them were killed with the sword that came out of the mouth of the rider on the horse and all the birds gorged themselves on their flesh.*

What does the Bible mean by "the rest of them?" I believe this phrase refers to all who followed the anti-Christ and turned their backs on God — that is, all of the unredeemed.

11

The Battle of Armageddon

The entire tribulation period will be full of war, famine, plagues, destruction, pestilence, corruption, immorality, and violent deaths. It will all come to an end with the final battle: The Battle of Armageddon.

This battle will conclude the tribulation. All who have survived the end times and maintained their loyalty to the anti-Christ will meet their doom. The battle will be brief but bloody. Jesus will speak and all the unfaithful will perish, and their chances of eternal life in heaven will end. Their chance to ask forgiveness will be gone forever. The final chapter will have been written.

Revelation 19:11-14 says: *And I saw heaven open: and behold, a white horse, and He who sat upon it is called Faithful and True; and in righteousness He judges and wages war. And His eyes are a flame of fire, and upon His head are many diadems; and He has a name written upon Him which no one knows except Himself. And He is clothed with a robe dipped in blood; and His name is called The Word of God. And the armies which are in heaven, clothed in fine linen, white and clean were following Him on white horses.* At this time, the anti-Christ will order his army to stop fighting and turn their weapons toward the Lord, who will put His foot down on the Mount of Olives. It will then split in two (it is known that there is an actual fault line beneath the Mount of Olives).

The battle will last a day. Zechariah 14:3-5 tells us: *3. Then the LORD will go out and fight against those nations, as he fights in the day of battle. 4. On that day his feet will stand on the Mount of Olives, east of Jerusalem, and the Mount of Olives will be split in two from east to west, forming a great valley, with half of the mountain moving north and half moving south. 5. You will flee by my mountain valley, for it will extend to Azel. You will flee as you fled from the earthquake in the days of Uzziah king of Judah. Then the LORD my God will come, and all the holy ones with him.*

Then it will be over. Jesus Christ will come as He promised, before mankind destroys itself. The carnage will be overwhelming; those who are not killed in the battle will be slain by the Word of God. Revelation 20:15 says: *And from his mouth comes a sharp sword, so that with it He may smite the nations; and He will rule them with a rod of iron; and He treads the wine press of the fierce wrath of God, the Almighty, and on His robe and on His thigh He has a name written; "King of Kings and Lord of Lords."*

I don't believe an actual sword will come out of the mouth of Jesus, but rather that His words will be as sharp as a sword and when He speaks; His words will be so incisive that the thousands of people who have denied Him will die instantly.

The following is an outline of the aforementioned events, listed in chronological order:

- The anti-Christ will defile the temple and take his seat. Israel will realize that she has been deceived — that he is not the messiah.

- The Israelites will flee to the mountains of Jordan (expected to be named Petra) where they will receive divine protection (Matthew: 24:15-22 and Revelation 12:6). (This means the Israelites who have accepted Jesus as the messiah will be sent to the mountains of Jordan and will be protected from the anti-Christ and his army who wants to destroy them)

- The anti-Christ will set up a system [to place the monetary markings on either the hand or the forehead for people to buy and sell] and begin persecuting all who do not accept the system (Ephesians: 13:16). (This was explained in an earlier chapter regarding anti-Christ forcing people to bow to him and take the mark)

- The northern army alliance (Gog-Magog) will attack Israel while simultaneously moving south into Africa. The West will most likely respond by deploying nuclear weapons.

- Israel may use both thermonuclear and neutron devices against the coalition, which might be comprised of Egypt, Russia, Iran, Iraq and Syria (Ezekiel 39:6).

- Economic chaos, food shortages, famine, and plagues will beset the earth's population as the war keeps escalating.

- A third of all ships, submarines, and sea life will be destroyed.

- A third of all fresh water will be poisoned.

- One fourth of the earth's population will be eradicated.

- The leaders of the East will join their forces, forming a 200-million-man army. A nuclear attack may be launched against the West.

- By this time, more than half of mankind will have perished. A third of the celestial light (from the sun, moon and stars) will be blocked due to the debris from the bombs and fires (Isaiah 13:9-10).

- Brutal demons will be released from a bottomless pit.

- The war of Armageddon will begin.

- The battles will begin in Jehoshaphat, the Jordan Valley, the Mountains of Moab, Edom and Bozrah.

- Upon his return, Christ will destroy the armies as He sets his foot down on the Mount of Olives.

- A huge battle will take place as it is written in Isaiah 24:1-23, 34:1-17 and Ezekiel 39:6.

- Christ will make changes to the earth so that once again, it will be able to nourish and sustain life. He will then gather all surviving Jews to be judged at Sinai, and all surviving gentiles to be judged at Jehoshaphat Valley.

- Finally, our Lord and Savior will restore order and it is written in Isaiah 65:20: *No more will there be in it an infant who lives but a few days, or an old man who does not live out his days: for the youth will die at the age of one hundred and the one who does not reach the age of one hundred shall be thought accursed.*

This last sentence refers to life during the "millennium period." The curse that dominated the earth will be lifted and a human's life span will be as in the days before the flood. Individual lives will last a thousand years. However, children will be born during this time. These children will be born into a sinful world. Even though Satan will be in the pit, the nature of the world will still be sinful and children will have to choose whether or not they will serve Jesus. It is difficult for me to think that children living during this time — all of whom will have Christian parents — will turn their backs on God. But since sin will still exist, there will still be rebellion. Those who do not choose to serve Jesus will be serving Satan; there is no middle ground. So those who choose rebellion will not live for even a hundred years, for they will be cursed. Man will still have free will, and therefore may choose to reject God and believe Satan's lie about Him.

At the end of a thousand years, Satan will be released for a very short time and be allowed to deceive the world again.

The following is an outline of the three major wars:

The first war will be between the northern army (which could be Russia and her allies) and Israel. This will take place either before or during the first 3½ years of the tribulation period. God will intercede and the northern army will be wiped out. This is described in Ezekiel 38:1 – 39:16.

The second war will be known as the Battle of Armageddon. It will be waged between the followers of the anti-Christ and God. It will take place in Jerusalem at the end of the seven-year tribulation period. Jesus Christ will come down from heaven and eliminate an army of more than 200 million men. This is when the anti-Christ and the False Prophet will be cast alive into the Lake of Fire. Satan will be bound in the bottomless pit for a thousand years (Revelation 20:1-3).

The third war will take place between God and Satan after the millennium period. God will release Satan from the pit one last time. Satan will then deceive millions of those who were born during the millennium. These people will form an army and attempt to defeat the believers and God by surrounding Jerusalem. God will send fire down from heaven, killing them all. God will then cast Satan into the Lake of Fire, where he will be tormented forever.

In John 3:3, Jesus says: *I tell you the truth; no one can see the kingdom of God unless he is born again. Flesh gives birth to flesh, but spirit gives birth to spirit.*

Because we were all born of flesh and blood, we can't be sure that God is there. We can see evidence of His existence everywhere. But we can't know who He is on a personal level until we know him spiritually. To receive spiritual birth, you need to accept the idea that Jesus Christ came to this earth and was sacrificed on the cross for every sin we have committed. He did this so that we might have a relationship with Him and receive eternal life. To have your name written in the Lamb's Book of Life, you must admit that you need Jesus and receive the gift of pardon He offers you.

In chapter 9, you were offered an opportunity to accept Jesus as your personal Savior. If you have not yet made that decision, I encourage you to make it now.

I'm looking forward to meeting you, either when the trumpet sounds, in heaven or at the beginning of the millennium when I return with the saints after Jesus' Glorious Appearing.

May God bless you and send His angels to watch over you. May the Holy Spirit give you courage, strength, and endurance. May He fill you with peace and His love.

12

Hope

THERE IS HOPE!

Right now, you are most likely experiencing grief, loss, frustration, confusion, and anguish. Perhaps you have even lost the will to live. It is likely that some of your family members and friends have suddenly disappeared, or possibly died as a result of the cataclysmic events that unfolded after the rapture of the church. Life as you know it has been changed — drastically changed forever.

Even if you find yourself wanting to "end it all," please DON'T. I can assure you that those who have miraculously disappeared are not dead but ALIVE. They are in their permanent home in heaven with Jesus and they are praying for you right now. Yes, they know you are here and they have been praying that you will reach an understanding of the truth. The Bible says, "The truth shall set you free." Undoubtedly, you want freedom from the anguish you are experiencing. You want answers and you've come to the right place because this book will provide them. But above all, I want you to know that you can, once again, see the family and friends who have vanished from this earth! And the way you may do so is so simple. All you have to do is accept the idea that God loves you – loves you so much that He made sure this book would fall in your hands so that you might know the truth. There is no time to waste, so please don't delay.

Unfortunately, horrible events are going to take place during the next few years. These events have been recorded in Revelation, the last book of the Bible. This book can be very confusing, so I have written this handbook to help you understand the chain of events that will take place after the rapture of the church. The wonderful part of all this is that you can still choose Jesus as your savior. I know you've heard of Him. Until now, you have probably believed that the idea of Jesus Christ and the rapture was all nonsense, and you wanted nothing to do with it. Maybe you didn't even believe in God — or you just didn't believe that God could love you. After all, there are millions of people on this earth, so why would He have any special feelings for you? Well, I'm telling you that He does! And as I mentioned before, you have family and friends in heaven praying for you RIGHT NOW.

Yes, God exists, and so does Satan. Satan hates and despises you and will whisper in your ear, telling you to throw down this book and run... run fast and don't look back. Why would he do this? Because he knows that if you run and turn your back on the truth, then he has you. You belong to him unless and until you make a decision to follow Jesus. Jesus has already paid the price for your sins. So there is no need to think you are so unworthy and so undesirable that Jesus couldn't love you. None of us are worthy. No one. He loves us anyway.

Jesus died on the cross so His blood would redeem us all. You can't clean yourself up enough to enter His presence. But when you pray and ask for His forgiveness, He will forgive you and you will be washed clean in His eyes. Your name will be written in "the Lamb's book of life" and regardless of what happens during the next few years, you will be a child of the King of kings and Lord of lords.

Since I don't know whether you are reading this book before or after the rapture has taken place, I don't know whether or not you have already experienced any of the events mentioned in this book. God gave us an outline to follow so we would know what to expect. Many of the plagues and horrific events I describe in this book will torment only those who have not repented and accepted Jesus Christ as the Son of God. But there will also be horrible earthquakes and other events from which you will not be protected. If you want eternal life in heaven, you must make a decision. And you *will* make a decision, whether or not you realize it. Because squandering your opportunity for everlasting life with our Father in heaven is, in effect, choosing eternal damnation. Satan doesn't want you to know this and right now he will do everything in his power to confuse you. He seeks only to devour and destroy.

If you survive the next few years, you will have the opportunity to live on this earth in a peaceful, loving environment for one thousand years. This period is known as the millennium, a time when Jesus and saints will reign on this earth. The earth will be renewed from all the devastation it has suffered from wars, plagues and earthquakes. When the millennium period begins, Jesus will descend from heaven to destroy the enemy forces on this earth. Then your loved ones who vanished in the rapture will come down to the earth and — if you have accepted Jesus as your savior — you will be reunited with them for the millennium period. After a thousand years, God will once again deal with all the evil that has entered the world during this time. Then we will all live together in peace forever and ever. No more wars. No more tears. What a glorious time that will be.

I have written this book for you. I want you to know there is HOPE. I don't know whether or not you will make it through the next few years or even the next few hours. But I do know that by making a decision to follow Jesus Christ, you will be with Him forever. Even if you lose your life here on earth, your life in heaven will be eternal — free from evil and free from darkness.

Use this book as a guide. It will enable you to recognize prophesied events as they unfold. As they play out, you will know in your heart that our Father in heaven is the one true God who has already related His plans in advance. The world leader who emerges during the tribulation period will be a cunning, deceptive and seductive person who will gain respect and admiration as he brings a false sense of peace to the world.

Don't be deceived. And don't despair. THERE IS HOPE.

13

The Millennium

It may be difficult for us to imagine living past a hundred years, let alone a thousand. However, after the seven-year tribulation period, saints from heaven will join those here on earth and reign with Jesus for a thousand years; a period known as "The Millennium." I believe that when the earth is changed and renewed, all diseases will be eradicated. The Bible says it will be a peaceful time, and the lion will lie down with the lamb. I interpret this as meaning that wild animals will not be a threat to us and we will have no worries about food or shelter. During this time, Satan will be chained in the pit. Believers who have survived the tribulation will live throughout the thousand-year period. People will replenish the earth with offspring, since marriages will still exist. The children brought into this world will eventually face the choice of whether to accept Jesus as their savior or rebel against Him. Although it will be a peaceful society and Satan will be chained in the pit, children will still be born with a sinful nature and have one hundred years to repent and accept Christ as their Lord. If they don't do so, they will die. If they do choose to serve Christ, they will be able to continue their lives on earth until the end of the Millennium period. Isaiah 65:20 says: *No more shall an infant from there live but a few days, nor an old man who has not fulfilled his days; for the child shall die one hundred years old, but the sinner being one hundred years old shall be accursed.*

In Revelation 20:4, we read: *I saw thrones on which were seated those who had been given authority to judge. And I saw the souls of those who had been beheaded because of their testimony for Jesus and because of the word of God. They had not worshipped the beast or his image and had not received his mark on their foreheads or their hands. They came to life and reigned with Christ a thousand years.*

The Millennium period will be followed by the "White Throne Judgment." This is described in a powerful passage of scripture. All those who have denied Christ will be consumed by dread and agony, for they will know the truth and it will be too late.

According to John, these are all the unsaved who have ever lived, now brought up from the grave and Hades to come before God and be judged. Revelation 20:12-13 says: *"They were judged, each one according to his works."* And Luke 8:17 tells us: *There is nothing hidden that will not be disclosed, and nothing concealed that will not be known or brought out into the open.*

After the unsaved are judged, another book is opened: the BOOK OF LIFE! In Revelation 20:15, John says: *"Anyone not found written in the Book of Life was cast into the lake of fire.* The idea of such a horrible eternal existence almost defies contemplation; it is hard to understand and accept.

However, throughout the Bible, God has given us every opportunity to know the truth and have our names written in the Lamb's Book of Life. If you are a believer in Christ, you will NOT stand before God at the White Throne of Judgment. Only those who have rejected Him will have to endure that.

Revelation 21 says: *Then I saw a new heaven and new earth, for the first heaven and first earth had passed away and there was no longer a sea.* The Holy City of Jerusalem will come down from heaven. We will have a new earth that will be changed and transformed, more beautiful than the Garden of Eden. There will no longer be a curse upon the earth. The trees will bear great fruit and the earth will be full of splendor.

We will live forever in this paradise. In the world as we know it, we can hardly imagine such a place. Our world today is ridden with disease, corruption, death and destruction. Some might scoff at the notion of a world of peace, dismissing the idea as a fairy tale. Many will turn their backs on the truth because of their lack of faith. But most of the Bible's prophecies have already come to pass; the only ones that haven't are the ones yet to come when the rapture takes place. Although this holy book was written thousands of years ago, its truth has been proven time and again. Don't get caught up in lies and misleading doctrines. If you want the truth, look in the Bible and you will find it.

I firmly believe that the Word of God, the Holy Bible, is the guide that God has given us to live by so that we may anticipate and prepare for these future events.

This book is a guide to help those left behind after the rapture of the church. My hope is that you have read this book before the rapture so that you can avoid the horror I have described. My prayer is that if the rapture has already taken place, you will keep this book close to you at all times so that you'll be able to interpret and understand the events unfolding around you, and anticipate the ones to come. Take this moment to say a prayer and ask Jesus to reveal His truth to you. Your prayers are your communication with God, who loves you and wants a relationship with you. You can speak to Him from your heart, for He knows your thoughts even before you voice them aloud. There is no need to wonder what to say or how to say it because He already knows your thoughts and feelings. He is waiting for you to approach Him in faith and ask Him to be your Savior and Lord.

14

How It All Began

Why are the Muslims and the Jews engaged in a war that never ends? What is the reason for this discord between the nations?

Genesis tells us that it all began when God bestowed a blessing upon Abraham and Sarah and promised them a son. The blessing was not only that Sarah (formerly known as Sarai) would be a mother of many nations, but that God would establish a covenant between them (Genesis 17:19).

Sarah had been barren for so many years that she had given up the hope of ever having a son. So she suggested that Abraham take their maidservant, Hagar, to be his wife and have a son with her. Sarah was aging and consumed with guilt for failing to bear a son for her husband. So when Abraham was 86 years old, he turned to Hagar, who was from Egypt. Genesis 16:1-4 states that: *1. Now Sarai, Abram's wife, had borne him no children. But she had an Egyptian maidservant named Hagar; 2. so she said to Abram, "The LORD has kept me from having children. Go, sleep with my maidservant; perhaps I can build a family through her." Abram agreed to what Sarai said. 3. So after Abram had been living in Canaan ten years, Sarai his wife took her Egyptian maidservant Hagar and gave her to her husband to be his wife. 4. He slept with Hagar and she conceived.*

When Hagar learned that she was pregnant, her relationship with Sarah became troubled. It is clear that

Sarah was jealous and that she became unkind to Hagar, which in turn caused Hagar to despise Sarah. There was an old Assyrian marriage contract stipulating that if, within two years, a wife had not produced offspring for her husband, she could buy a maidservant to produce children in her stead, and afterward, she could sell the maidservant.

It is clear that Sarah suggested this arrangement without realizing how it would affect her. She was anxious to provide her husband with an heir and forgot the promise from God, or perhaps she simply didn't believe it would really happen since she had long since aged beyond her childbearing years. So she chose a young maidservant to produce the child she thought she could never have. How she regretted that decision later!

Hagar tried to escape this situation by running away, but Genesis 16:9-12 tells us that one of God's angels came to her: *9. Then the angel of the LORD told her, "Go back to your mistress and submit to her." 10. The angel added, "I will so increase your descendants that they will be too numerous to count." 11. The angel of the LORD also said to her: "You are now with child and you will have a son. You shall name him Ishmael, for the LORD has heard of your misery. 12. He will be a wild donkey of a man; his hand will be against everyone and everyone's hand against him, and he will live in hostility toward all his brothers."* Thus Hagar understood that she had to return to Abraham and Sarah and bear this child. The angel's description of him as a "wild donkey" indicated that he would be a difficult child and hard to control. But he would also be a father of a great nation.

After some years had passed and Abraham was ninety-nine years old, three angels came to visit him. In

Genesis 18:10-15, it is written: *10. Then the LORD said, "I will surely return to you about this time next year, and Sarah your wife will have a son." Now Sarah was listening at the entrance to the tent, which was behind him. 11. Abraham and Sarah were already old and well advanced in years and Sarah was past the age of childbearing. 12. So Sarah laughed to herself as she thought, "After I am worn out and my master is old, will I now have this pleasure?" 13. Then the LORD said to Abraham, "Why did Sarah laugh and say, 'Will I really have a child, now that I am old?' 14. Is anything too hard for the LORD? I will return to you at the appointed time next year and Sarah will have a son. 15. Sarah was afraid, so she lied and said, "I did not laugh." But he said, "Yes, you did laugh."*

I think this passage is quite humorous. Imagine Sarah behind the tent entrance, listening to what the angel was saying. The custom during that time was for women to absent themselves from meetings between men. But Sarah was curious and wanted to know what the angel was saying, so she listened. She overheard the angel telling Abraham that he would have a son with her within a year. When Sarah heard this, she laughed, thinking the idea preposterous. She was ninety years old! God probably saw humor in it also, but wanted the event to reveal a miracle from Him and it did. Think of a time in your life when you wanted to share some good news with someone you loved, and the joy you felt when you finally had the opportunity. I imagine God enjoyed this just as much. I believe that since we are made in God's image, we can attribute our qualities and emotions to our Lord. Our love, compassion, humor, and creativity are from the one who has all these qualities and more. I imagine that He laughs harder than we do, and I don't doubt that He loves more than we could ever love. I believe that He gets sad and angry just as we do.

Returning to the topic of Ishmael, we remember that originally he was Abraham's only son and didn't like the idea of another son who would divert his father's attention. When Sarah became pregnant, he began acting up and misbehaving. When Isaac was born, there was much festivity and attention given to the new child. When Isaac was being weaned, there was a celebratory feast, and Ishmael behaved so badly toward Isaac that Sarah insisted that he and Hagar return to the latter's native country of Egypt.

This troubled Abraham because he loved Ishmael also, but he trusted that God would oversee the situation and sent them away. Hagar was beside herself and cried out to God as she took her son away. God had compassion for Hagar, but Ishmael became bitter, nonetheless. He felt that the special blessing given to Sarah should have been given to his mother instead. He grew hateful and rejected the God of Abraham.

Hagar's return to Egypt marked the beginning of Ishmael's insecurity and hostility toward the Jews, which eventually gave rise to the Islamic movement. Spiritual descendants of Ishmael became followers of Islam. Three primary words in Arabic are: 1) Allah, or God; 2) Islam, or submission; and 3) Qu-ran or Koran, the Book of Law. Ishmael's descendants became Arabian nomads or Bedouins.

Muslims believe that it is through their law alone that they must earn their salvation. They dismiss the idea that they can simply accept Jesus as their savior and be saved by grace. This is heresy to them. They consider it blasphemy against God to believe that He had a son who died for our sins. Muslims still live under the old law. We, however, can be confident that we are saved by grace through Jesus Christ. Muslims are very aware of Jesus and do not deny his existence, but they consider him a mere prophet who did not rise from the dead.

Followers of Islam have no personal relationship with God nor any sense of eternal security. The only ones with eternal security are martyrs. Does that shed some light on what is happening in the world today – specifically, on why there are so many suicide bombers in the Middle East?

At any rate, there is no denying that the conflict between the Muslims and the Jews has persisted to this day, and their battle will not end until the tribulation.

If this book has been informative and helpful to you, please share it with others.

Additional Information and References

If you wish to obtain more copies of this book you may order online on my website

www. Keithandvickihallett.com

Suggested Books and websites:

MarkBeast.com

Timlahaye.com

Biblegateway.com

http://www.geocities.com/tiasmemory/index.html

For Grief counseling:

Griefshare.org

http://brokenheartslivinghope.homestead.com

Books:

The Invincible Power of Praise by James R. Swanson

www.ingramcontent.com/pod-product-compliance
Lightning Source LLC
LaVergne TN
LVHW011213080426
835508LV00007B/758